# DAWN TO TWILIGHT

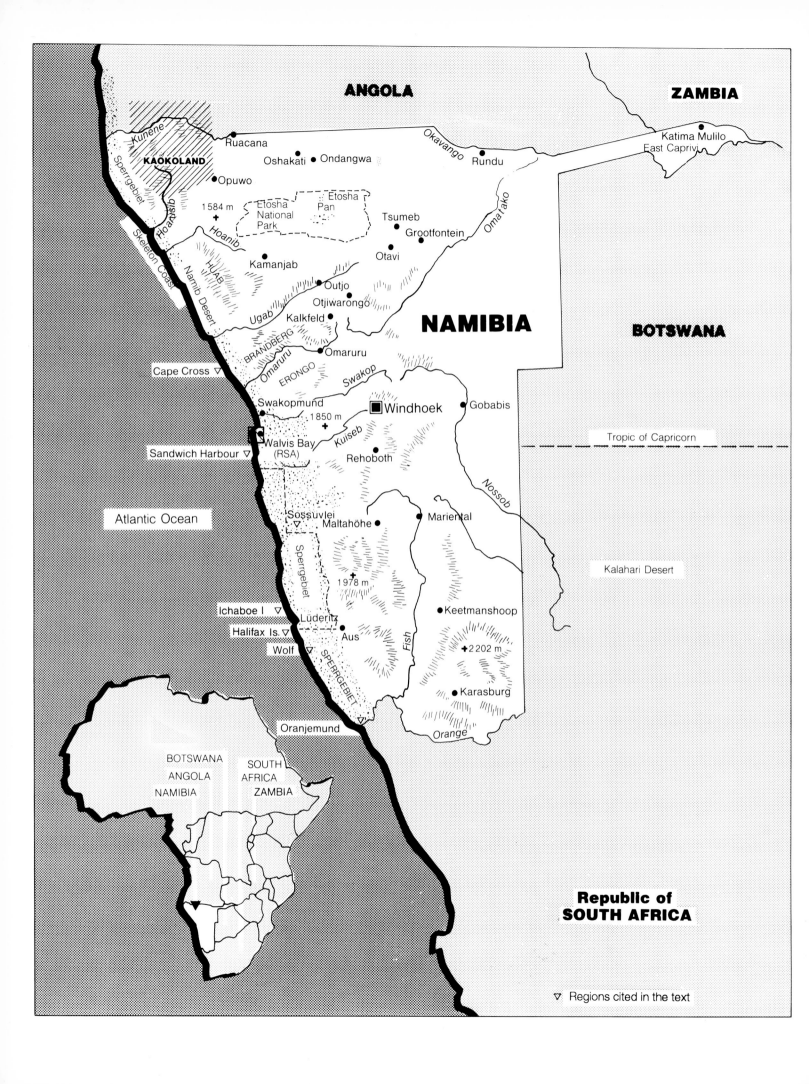

# NAMIB

## DAWN TO TWILIGHT

SYLVIE BERGEROT

ERIC ROBERT

Written in collaboration with
Dr JEAN-PAUL ROUX
With maps and illustrations by
Suzanne Roux

SOUTHERN
BOOK PUBLISHERS

We understand and define a desert primarily by what it lacks: it has little rain; scarcely any rivers; few or no inhabitants; little animal life; no arable soil; a minimum of plant cover. We all agree on one point, a desert is an extremely arid region. An area will usually be classified as a desert if the annual evaporation is at least double the annual rainfall or if the latter is less than 150 mm.

Most of the deserts of the world are located in two symmetrical belts situated around 30° latitude north and south of the equator. In the northern hemisphere, if we follow the 30th parallel from east to west, we cross successively the Sahara and the Libyan Deserts, the north of the Arabian Desert, the Iranian Desert and the Thar Desert on the Indo-Pakistanian border; then on the American continent, the arid region of Baja California, the Mojave and

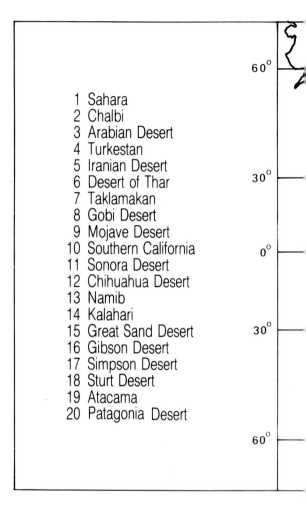

1 Sahara
2 Chalbi
3 Arabian Desert
4 Turkestan
5 Iranian Desert
6 Desert of Thar
7 Taklamakan
8 Gobi Desert
9 Mojave Desert
10 Southern California
11 Sonora Desert
12 Chihuahua Desert
13 Namib
14 Kalahari
15 Great Sand Desert
16 Gibson Desert
17 Simpson Desert
18 Sturt Desert
19 Atacama
20 Patagonia Desert

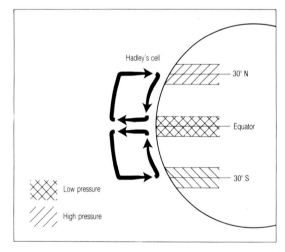

Hadley's cell

30° N

Equator

30° S

Low pressure

High pressure

the desert of Sonora. The 30th parallel of latitude south of the equator takes us successively across the Namib and the Kalahari in Africa, the Australian deserts of Gibson, Victoria, Simpson and Sturt, until we finally reach the southern part of the Atacama Desert on the west coast of South America.

This zonal distribution of the principal deserts of the world is caused by the presence of two high pressure belts on either side of the equator. Along the equator, at the heart of a permanent low pressure zone, air tends to rise. As it gains altitude the air cools down and condensation occurs, causing the characteristic

equatorial and intertropical climate. This air, cooled and dried, tends to descend along the 30° N and 30° S parallels. In its descent, the air warms up as the pressure increases, but cannot reabsorb humidity. Along these latitudes, we have a quasi-permanent anticyclonic zone of stable, dry air which contributes to the aridity of these regions. The air finally returns at low altitude in the direction of the equatorial low pressure system generating the trade winds. This symmetrical atmospheric circulation is known as Hadley's cell.

The principal source of atmospheric water is evaporation from the ocean surface. So it may seem strange to find arid regions and deserts along the coast of a great ocean, for example Baja California, the Atamaca Desert and the

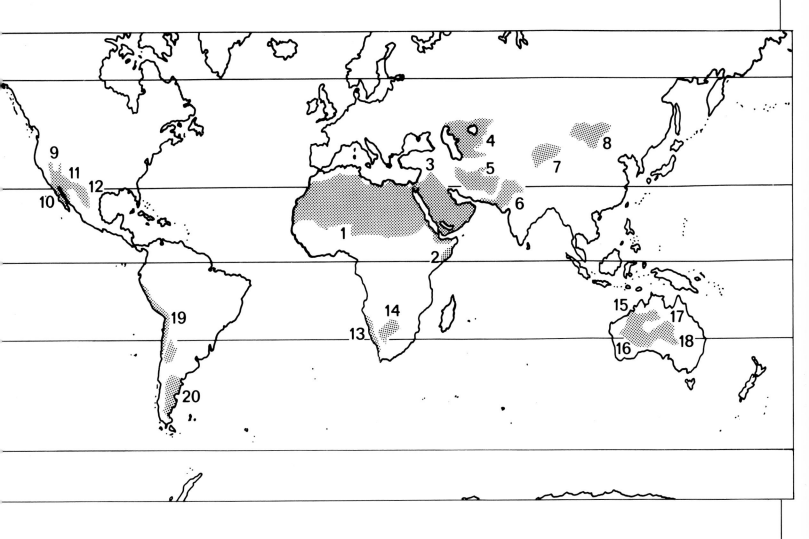

Namib. These three areas have a number of points in common. All three are situated at the latitude of the high pressure systems generated by Hadley's cells, along the western coastlines of large continents, and are bathed by cold currents (the California current, the Humbolt current and the Benguela current respectively). These cold currents reinforce the aridity of these areas. Upon contact with the cold ocean, the air cools and a zone of temperature inversion is created. This cooling causes the condensation of atmospheric humidity in fog along the coast and therefore prevents rainfall inland. In turn, the fog limits the heating of the ocean surface by the sun and impedes further evaporation.

Outside the desert belts along the high pressure systems, remoteness from the oceans explains the presence of deserts at the centre of large continents for example the Taklamakan and the Gobi Deserts in central Asia. A high mountain range can also constitute a barrier to ocean humidity, as when a mass of humid air encounters a slope, it is pushed to a higher altitude and the loss of pressure and temprature precipitates rain on the windward side of the range. Thus, the air reaching the other side is dry. This factor contributes to the aridity of some deserts such as those of Iran, the Gibson Desert in Australia, the Patagonian Desert at the foot of the Andes and the Mojave in California.

The main characteristic of desert ecosystems is a very limited supply of water, which is both infrequent and unpredictable.

# NAMIBIA DAWNS
## SOUNDLESS IN MIST

AT SUNRISE THE NAMIB
SEEMS A PRIMORDIAL VISION OF THE BEGIN-
NING OF TIME, FOG SHROUDING
THE SOFT LIGHT THAT SLOWLY
AWAKENS THE DESERT

# THE NAMIB DESERT

The Namib desert extends along the south-west coast of Africa in a high pressure zone generated by Hadley's cells. The desert covers a coastal area of approximately 1 900 km long between the Olifants River mouth in the Cape Province of South Africa and the district of Namibe (originally Mocamedes) in southern Angola. It is crossed by two perennial rivers, the Kunene and the Orange River, which mark the northern and southern borders of Namibia. To the south of the Orange River, the desert is usually less than 50 km wide; in Namibia, along the 1 400 km between the Orange and the Kunene Rivers, the Namib, stretching to the Great Escarpment to the east, reaches an altitude of about 1 000 m and a maximum width of 200 km. This central part of the desert is the most arid.

The elephants killed by anthrax attracts starving young lions.

This region has a great landscape diversity: immense gravel plains (hamada), dune fields, sand seas, inselbergs, chains of rocky hills, massive mountains to the east, salt flats, dry river beds, as well as the mouths of two permanent rivers which constitute the only oases in this endless aridity.

## THE BENGUELA SYSTEM

Above the Atlantic Ocean there exists a permanent anticyclone at 30°S in summer and 26°S in winter. This anticyclone causes southerly winds along the coast of the Namib Desert. The wind generates surface currents; as a consequence of the relatively stable meteorological conditions, a surface current flows NNW up the Namib coast. It is not a fast current, flowing between 6 and 30 m per hour. Yet this current is but one aspect of the Benguela "system" which is also characterized by powerful "upwellings". This welling up of deep, cold ocean water to the surface significantly lowers the surface temperature along the coast. As a result, surface temperature is between 5°C and 8°C lower than water temperature at the same latitude further offshore, and temperatures of 12°C to 13°C are not rare at the Tropic of Capircorn. The presence of this mass of cold water profoundly influences the climate of the Namib Desert, resulting in moderate temperatures along the coast and limited rainfall. Temperature inversion at lower atmospheric levels, also a consequence of the cold water, creates favourable conditions for the formation of fog which fills the important ecological function of providing the main source of moisture for most species of plants and animals along the coast.

## CLIMATE

The Namib is a rather temperate desert. Temperatures above 40°C in the shade are rare and the annual average maximum temperatures is about 30°C; 12°C to 15°C the average minimum. As a result of sunshine, temperatures at ground level frequently exceed 60°C

Amazing rain in the Namib sand dunes.

and at times 70°C. Temperatures can drop below 0°C by the end of the night in the central part of the desert. These drastic differences in ambient temperature render life particularly difficult for both plants and animals.

The Namib is very arid. The least dry area, the foot of the Great Escarpment to the east, receives an annual rainfall of only about 100 mm. Precipitation progressively diminishes across the width of the Namib from east to west and along the coast the average does not exceed 12 to 15 mm. The southern sector, particularly the area south of the Orange River, receives winter rainfall, while the northern sector is distinguished by summer showers. In the central area, rainfall is very scarce and not seasonal. It is not unusual for a locality to receive no rain at all for several consecutive years and then to receive several times the yearly average in one or two downpours.

The fog provides an important source of moisture in the coastal areas, which is in fact more predictable and reliable than rain. The fog is at its densest at ground level between 300 and 600 m above sea level, producing important condensation on the hillsides. During the night the fog can extend up to 50 km inland, often lingering during the morning but normally dissipating before noon.

Southerly and SSW winds prevail along the coast and blow between 40% and 60% of the time; they are also the strongest. They are responsible for the transport and the accumulation of sand in the dune fields and the sand seas. The westerly winds are more moderate and cause the penetration of fog far inland. Easterly and north-easterly winds are hot and desiccating and when they gust in the central part of the desert, the humidity level falls precipitously to between 5% and 0% while the ambient temperature rises several degrees in minutes. These winds are more frequent in winter.

Winds in the Namib Desert fill important functions both in the shaping of the landscape and in the ecology. It is the wind which carries and accumulates the sand and blows the fine elements from the surface of the plains, leaving behind only rocks and gravel. Loaded with

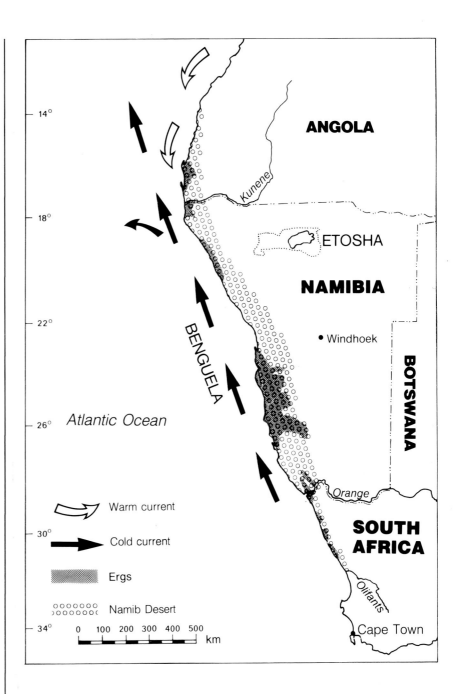

sand, the wind erodes and polishes the rocks. The wind also distributes detritus of organic matter into the heart of the desert, providing food and nutrients for animals even in areas naturally devoid of all vegetation.

15

*A*t the edge of the desert, near the central part of the Great

Escarpment, erosion has carved huge reliefs. It has taken several

million years for water to excavate canyons such as this one of the

Fish River. Today only a thin trickle of water runs generally, and it

is difficult to imagine the floods necessary to erode away a valley.

In a mineral universe, where all seems hostile and wears the face of

death, life is a land of faraway dreams. Maybe a secret beauty lurks

in the desolation.

*T*he eternal fog, the force of the surf and violent currents that throw boats up on the shore have made a sinister reputation for the northern coast of the desert, called by sailors, Skeleton Coast. The Portuguese explorer, Diego Cao, was the first European to land on this inhospitable coast in 1486. He erected a cross which served as a landmark for boats headed toward the Cape of Good Hope. The many shipwrecks tell tragic stories of the ill-fated, whose bones whiten in the sun.

IN THE DUNES OF GOBABEB,

*A*t the foot of the dunes, this « white lady » of the family *Hetero podidae* builds nests reaching 30 to 40cm into the sand. The nests are in fact tubes, the inner sides of which are constructed of sand and silk. An elaborate trap camouflages the entrance to the nest. During the night this spider hunts prey around her nest, mostly insects, small lizards and scorpions. Very territorial, she attacks other spiders encroaching on her domain, including her own young. Her primary predators are other white ladies, gerbils and birds.

*A* shocking contrast opposes the poverty of Himba

life and the people's passion for jewellery and adornment of the

body. At dawn, sheltered in their hut, the women paint their

bodies with an ointment that gives their skin the characteristic

red colour.

# KAOKOLAND
## IN THE LAND OF THE HIMBA

Kaokoland, situated in the north-west of the country, is bounded to the north by the Kunene River which marks the frontier with Angola, to the east by Ovamboland and Etosha Park, and to the south by the Hoanib River, which divides Damaraland. The Skeleton Coast Park, on the western coast, provides a boundary, parallel to the Atlantic, 32 km into the interior. In size, Kaokoland is about 50,000 km², measuring 265 km north to south and 240 km east to west.

The country can be characterized geographically as highlands and the western plains. The average height of the highlands is about 1200m, the highest point reaching 2000m in the north. These mountains are part of various geological eras, the oldest stratum being granitic gneiss as much as 2000 million years old. They are, for the most part, oriented north-south, but a few chains run south-east to north-west. These latter divide the tributaries flowing north into the Kunene and those flowing south into the Hoarusib. These rivers are dry most of the time, but the absence of running water is compensated for by the many permanent springs and by subterranean water.

All the rivers rise in the highlands, where an abrupt rocky escarpment to the west dominates the desert plains of the pro-Namib. These expanses are covered with sand, or gravel and stones, and crossed by wide dry river beds which provide the sole support for the growth of trees such as the mopane and the acacia. In a westerly direction, the sparse vegetation of bush and annual plants becomes progressively scarcer as one approaches the long, narrow strip of the Namib Desert.

When the summer east winds bring the long-awaited precipitation, the rivers of the highlands transform in a few hours into torrents, bringing water to the pro-Namib. The Kunene, normally 80m wide, can be as wide as 300m during this season and it inundates the plains. Tempera-

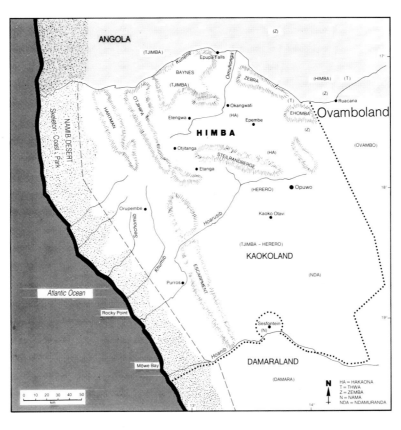

tures also become more moderate, bringing relief after the 40°C of the summer months.

The Himbas, estimated at pop. 7,000, live principally in the highlands where the climate is more favourable. The semi-desert bush cannot support a large herd, thus necessitating a nomadic life. The culture is closely linked to the herd religiously, socially and economically. And it is possession of the herd which determines the two social stratas of the Ovahona, rich proprietors of many head of cattle, and the Ovasyona, modest owners of small stock. A man with no animals is called Motjimba, in reference to the Tjimba who are grouped in two : after the Hereros fled to Angola and became known as the Himbas, a small group remained in Kaokoland, living as hunters and gatherers. Compared to the antbear which must hunt and dig for its food, they are called Tjimba. Once the Himbas returned to Kaokoland, the Tjimbas decided to leave their mountain refuge for the minor work of herding, yet still maintain their customary way of life. This group can be called Tjimba-Herero, being originally Herero who lost the pastoral model and assumed hunting and gathering as an alternative life. Conversely, there exists a "true" group of Tjimbas (Tjimba-Tjimba), discovered 20 years ago, who seem to be hunter-gatherers in origin and are of an entirely different race. There are approximately 150 and their derivation remains a mystery. The Himbas live for and believe in multiplying the herd and are remarkable herders. Synonymous with wealth, the herd does not represent commercial value, but rather is a status symbol. The Himbas subsist entirely on the herd, receiving grain, tobacco and knives from specific tribes in exchange for a few cows or goats.

Even during periods of social and climatic duress, or amidst cattle plague, the Himba have never turned to either agriculture or hired themselves out as labourers. Rather, they have continually sought to restore the herd.

*F*or aesthetic reasons, but also to protect them from the sun and cold, every morning the women patiently rub **otjize** on their bodies and hair. Kept in a small box of horn and skin, the red substance is extracted from a stone, hematite. Reduced to a powder and kneaded with fat, it acquires the consistency of a cream. Reserves are carefully guarded because there is only one quarry in Kaokoland, a few hours' or even a few days' trek from the village.

*H*airstyle fills an important social function and distinguishes boys and girls at an early age. Boys have shaven heads, except for a strip along the middle of their heads, which they allow to grow into a braid toward puberty. When they reach marriageable age, the braid is cut in two. Adoption of a hairstyle is celebrated in a profound ritual and marks membership of a social group.

## SUNK IN THE DUNES

Whataen sailing along the Namib coast, one realizes that land offers no firm refuge and no hope for survival. A curious feeling of betrayal by the earth haunts the man who hopes to walk these sands, where only death awaits. Nature seems to be keeping an appointment in hell for a final combat. The sea ceases where the desert begins, yet in time the shoreline shifts again. Images from another world, wrecked ships are sunk in the dunes. The ever present fog creates a strange aura, almost of gloom oppressing, as forms grow vague and disappear, sucked up by the white mist, and the apparition of a phantom ship takes us back into legendary times.

*T*he climate of the Namib Desert is determined by
Atlantic air refreshed by the cold current of the
Benguela system. The many penguins and seals profit
from the relatively cold ocean temperature. Their
presence at the peak of the Tropic of Capricorn and
beside a desert remains an arresting sight. The
penguins live on the many islets near shore and reign
supreme there.

*U*nder the influence of south-southwest winds due to a high pressure front in the South Atlantic, the Namib coast experiences the phenomenon known as "upwelling." Veritable food reservoirs, these upwellings occur in only 1/1000th of the world's ocean surface and attract large shoals of fish which themselves become prey for sea birds and marine mammals. Here is the riveting contrast of a desolate landscape bathed by an ocean swarming with life. An uninhabited hinterland thus is permitted an extraordinarily rich coast.

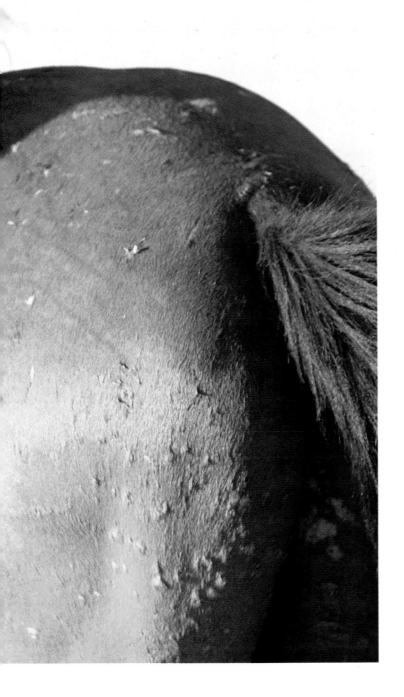

The horse, used to transport packs of sand in the mining town of Kolmanskop, was the companion of good fortune to the colonials at the beginning of the century. The army also called upon the cavalry during the war of pacification in which robust Hanovarians and Trackener made saddle horses for the soldiers of the Second Reich. The German defeat in 1915, then the closing of the Kolmanskop mines, led to the abandonment of these horses, which turned wild. Incredibly, they adapted to the extreme environment and can last 4 to 5 days without water, some seen to be still standing after 7.

*T*he women convene around the huts with their

babies. The men seem to have disappeared, as if to

make this moment possible. Laughter, childish babbling

and conniving sidelong glances speak the privilege of

the moment. The nursing child is inseparable from the

mother who lets him sleep on her knee or carries him

on her back wherever she goes.

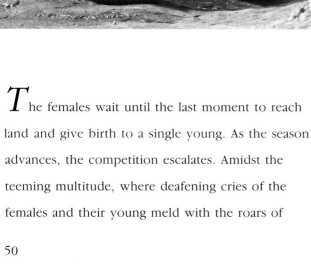

*T*he females wait until the last moment to reach land and give birth to a single young. As the season advances, the competition escalates. Amidst the teeming multitude, where deafening cries of the females and their young meld with the roars of

ferocious males defending their territories, certain seals are forced to give birth in a virtual battlefield. In the first moments of life, mother and young exchange the cries and mutual scents that will be the signs of recognition between them.

The females quickly return to the ocean to feed and within one week after birth the babies are left for several days at a time. On her return, the female seal must find her progeny in the midst of many thousand others.

$A$s a pastoral tribe, the Himbas migrate to ensure
survival of the herd, and go where grazing and water
are available. Sometimes the village settles for only one
or two days. Huts are constructed for temporary
habitation and so remain very rudimentary. The day of
departure, the women gather together their minimum
of personal possessions, a few goat or cow pelts, a few
cooking utensils and jewellery. Unwearying walkers,
the Himbas often march under an oppressive sun. Each
one walks at his or her own pace, so the village
departs and arrives in a loose order.

53

*T*he women gather together all the articles of daily life in small baskets they carry on their heads according to African custom. This little hat made of goat hide (**erembe**) is the distinguishing mark of a married woman. It can be lowered to the back of the head to free the crown for carrying water or packages during migration. The essential reserves of the village are, rather, strapped to a mule.

# IN THE UNRELENTING
# HEAT OF THE DESERT

THE HIGH SUN IN MID-AFTERNOON IS ALL-
ENCOMPASSING, INESCAPABLE;
ALL LIFE RESTS AND WAITS,
HOPING FOR RELIEF THAT COMES ONLY
IN ELUSIVE DREAMS.

The survival of plants and animals in the desert is largely dependent on the availability of water, the single most essential element for life. By its very scarcity, water is the main controlling factor of desert ecosystems. Yet we encounter an amazing diversity of life forms in the Namib Desert.

### ESCAPE FROM THE DESERT

The most common form of adaptation to the desert environment may seem paradoxical: the majority of plants and animals which occur in the desert do not actually live in this environment! Rather, many of them avoid the harshness of the desert by taking advantage of favourable micro-habitats or by migratory behaviour.

Grant's golden mole *(Emitalpa granti)* lives exclusively in the sand dunes of the Namib Desert. It is 8.5 cm in length, and totally blind. During the day it escapes the conditions of the desert by burrowing in the sand, often more than 50 cm down. At such depth the temperature is constant and moderate. Once night has fallen, the golden mole becomes active, re-emerges at about 21 h 00 and starts hunting. Because of the fluidity of sand, the mole's movements resemble those of a swimmer as it hunts crickets, beetles, other insects and even small geckos. The mole finds in its prey most of the water it needs to survive.

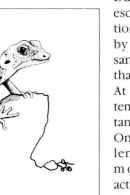

Rhoptropus afer

The palmato gecko *(Palmategecko rangei)*, like many other small animals of the Namib, also spends the day deeply buried in the sand and hunts on the surface of the dunes during the night. This gecko runs easily on the unstable dune sand with its webbed feet.

Many plants and animals, though, cannot escape completely the harsh conditions of the desert. Their survival thus depends upon morphological, physiological and behavioural

Pterocles namaqua

adaptations which enable them to tolerate the constraints of the desert environment.

Carnivores find in their prey between 60 and 70% of water and this covers most of their needs. Granivores such as the Namaqua sandgrouse *(Pterocles namaqua)*, on the other hand, derive very little water from their diet. Thus this bird must travel every day, up to 60 km, to reach water. The sandgrouse nests on the ground and the chicks are capable of foraging for themselves from the moment they hatch, yet under the guard of a parent. But because they are unable to fly, the chicks cannot reach water. The male sandgrouse possesses specialized breast feathers which absorb water like a sponge. He will immerse these feathers at a water source before flying back to the chicks dozens of kilometres away. The bird is capable of carrying 20 to 40 ml of water which the chicks drink avidly on his return.

The gemsbok exhibits an extraordinary tolerance for high temperatures. This animal, as well as the ostrich and springbok, orientates its body so that the least possible area is exposed to the sun during hot days. It also seeks out the crest of dunes to gain the maximum benefit of the breeze. When these strategies are insufficient and as long as the animal does not lack water, the gemsbok relies on panting and the evaporation of sweat to cool itself (as the majority of mammals do). Yet, when the animal is dehydrated and unable to produce sweat its body temperature rises. The gemsbok is exceptional in its capacity to sustain a body temperature of over 45°C, which is three degrees above the lethal point for most mammals. This tolerance of the gemsbok is due to the animal's adaptive capability to keep the temperature of its brain up to 3°C lower than that of its body.

The gemsbok achieves this thermoregulation by intense evaporation which cools the nasal membranes and the blood irrigating these membranes during panting. This cooled blood then flows into a network of blood vessels located not far from the base of the brain before returning to the body. The warm blood from the carotid arteries also passes through this network, the varotid rete, before entering the cerebral cavity. In the carotid rete, the small veins and arteries are tightly entwined and their warm arterial blood is cooled by the blood coming from the nasal cavity. Thus the blood entering the brain is several degrees cooler than the rest of the body.

The surface of the sand can reach temperatures above 70°C by mid-afternoon, yet a few centimetres above the sand, the temperature diminishes substantially due to the refreshing effect of the breeze. Diurnal terrestrial insects in the Namib generally have much longer legs than nocturnal species and can take advantage of this thermal gradient. In fact it is in the central Namib that we find the insect with proportionally the longest recorded legs, the tenebrionid *Cauricara phalangium*. This insect begins the day on folded legs, its body as close as possible to the ground warmed by the morning

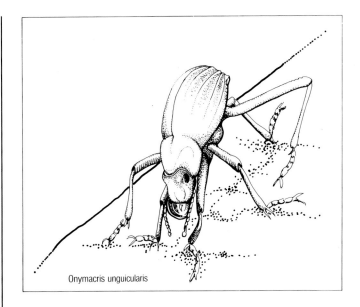
Onymacris unguicularis

sun. As the temperature rises, it gradually extends its stilt-like legs to keep its body in the breeze.

When the sand temperature rises, the lizard *Aporosaura anchietae* begins a thermoregulatory dance, alternately lifting its feet, two at a time, to cool them. If the temperature rises even further, this lizard disappears under the sand until later in the day. Other animals, such as the gecko *Rhoptropus afer* of the rocky plains, climb high rocks to find the refreshing breeze.

## THE FOG: SOURCE OF LIFE

Many animals in the Namib Desert have evolved with adaptive capabilities of using water from the fog. The beetle *Onymacris unguicularis* slowly emerges from its subterranean retreat when the fog moves into the dunes, and climbs toward the summit of the dune face where the condensation is densest. Once there it faces the breeze with a lowered head. Little by little the fog condenses on its back and drips down toward its mouth where the droplets are eagerly lapped up. Many other insects and reptiles profit from the fog, either collecting the tiny drops of condensation that form on the sand and the rocks, or licking up the condensation on their own bodies.

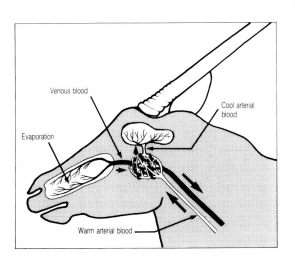

Venous blood

Cool arterial blood

Evaporation

Warm arterial blood

*E*ven in the middle of the desert, water exists. At
Sossusvlei, vegetation profits from underground water to
grow, and trees such as acacias seem to forget the harsh
surroundings. Other plants, called succulents, are adapted for
survival in a hostile environment. Certain ones, such as
aloes, insinuate themselves into the cracks of rocks to hide
from the fiery sun.

*I*f the underground water-table lowers, this is sufficient deprivation for a tree to die off. Only those survive which have found some form of adaptation. The tortuous shape of the *Moringa ovalifolia* and the arrogant silhouette of the *Pachypodium namaquam* seem to shout out victory.

# ADAPTIVE STRATEGIES

**P**lants encounter the same challenges as animals in surviving the desert environment. Seeds can withstand very long periods of dryness as well as periods of extreme temperature elevation without losing their power of germination. Their metabolism is suspended to such a point that it is difficult to consider them alive. Yet a sudden heavy rain-shower and the seeds spring to life. Annual plants then begin a race against time, developing extremely quickly, flowering and producing seeds before the sun dries them out again. The complete cycle from germination to seed production in these plants is very rapid, taking one to three weeks at most. The next generation of seeds will then wait many months for the next rain.

**Lichens**

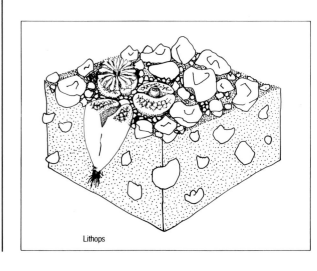

In the fog zone, condensation on the ground occurs regularly but the quantity of moisture deposited is often insufficient for plant growth. At the foot of the rocky hills facing west, plants and flowers are relatively luxuriant. In effect, the western faces of the hills and the surrounding rocks make an effective catchment area for the fog. The condensation occurring over a large surface area drains off and collects at the foot of the rocks, where the plants find a favourable micro-habitat richer in moisture than the surrounding desert.

## THE SUCCULENT FLORA

Some plants have developed specific forms of adaptation to tolerate conditions of extreme aridity. Water management remains the fundamental problem in the desert and certain plants are capable of remarkable economy: Just as the lizard *Aporosaura anchietae* can store water in the elastic diverticulys of its intestine, lots of desert plants are also capable of storing water. Known as succulents, these plants are quite well represented in the Namib Desert and have specialized organs for storing water situated in the trunk (*Pachypodium* and *Moringa*, for example), in the stem (the Euphorbias), in the leaves (*Zygophylum* and the *Mesembryanthemaceae*) or in the roots.

The succulent organs possess specialized cells which stretch to fill with water. The plant, then, can draw upon this reserve during long periods of drought. In addition, succulents have, in general, an extremely reduced foliage surface or, even, lose their leaves in the dry season. These strategies limit the loss of water by evaporation. The trunk or stem surface is often modified into a photosynthetic organ, thus certain species survive with almost no leaves whatsoever.

During photosynthesis all plants absorb carbon dioxide from the air and then, through complex biochemical reactions which require water and energy from the sun received through the chlorophyll pigments, the plants produce carbohydrates and oxygen. The absorbtion of carbon dioxide takes place in the stomata, specialized structures which normally open during the day, when photosynthesis occurs, and close during the night. Yet, in a desert environment, this normal process would result in a significant loss of water by evaporation through the open stomata. Succulents possess a quite different biochemical cycle which allows their stomata to remain closed during the heat of the day. The stomata of the succulents rather open at night, when the

Lithops

air is cool and the humidity level rises, conditions under which carbon dioxide can be absorbed without losing too much water. At night, without sunlight, photosynthesis is not possible though, but $CO_2$ is stored in the form of complex acids in the plant cells. Once day returns, the stomata closes and $CO_2$ is released by decarboxylation and then used for photosynthesis in the classical way. This process, called CAM (Crassulacean Acid Metabolism), is a little less efficient than the classical cycle but thanks to the economy of water CAM permits the succulents to survive in conditions that would otherwise forbid all vegetative growth. To combat high temperatures through exposure to the sun, certain desert species possess very light coloured, reflective bark (*Pachypodium lealii* and the quiver tree, *Aloe diohotoma*, for example). Other plants radically reduce the surface area exposed to the sun: the entirety of the plant may be subterranean, with the exception of one or two specialized leaves, which bloom at ground level. The succulent leaves are filled with water-loaded transparent tissues which transmit the light to the rest of the plant, just as a window open to the sky. This radical form of adaptation is found in the lithops (flowering stones) and the window plants (*Fenestraria*).

### THE IMPORTANCE OF FOG

What seems to be only a stony plain utterly bare in mid-afternoon, suddenly assumes verdant colour in the morning. On closer inspection, each stone, each little piece of gravel is observed to be covered with lichens. We are standing in a lichen field in the fog zone of the Namib Desert. Lichens are particularly sturdy plants thriving, of all plants, closest to the poles, at the highest altitudes and farthest into the deserts. Here, in the Namib, they resist well desiccation and high temperatures. When the humidity level rises they return to life for a few hours before drying out again in the sun.

In the large sand sea of the central Namib, only two species of perennial can survive the scarcity of precipitations : one is an herb stipagrostis sabulicola, and the other is a succulent,

*Trianthema hereroensis.* Both are capable of taking in moisture from the fog. The first possesses a lateral root system which can extend up to 20 m from the plant. It can absorb the condensation that occasionally forms on the surface of the dunes. The second, *Trianthema*, is capable of absorbing condensation through its leaves rather than through a complex root system.

Another plant of the Namib, the extraordinary *Welwitschia mirabilis*, combines these two techniques. This plant is a botanical curiosity and has to be classified separately. It is found only in the fog zone of the Namib Desert. The oldest living specimens are about 1 500 years old. The plant possesses one pair of tough "leaves" which are in a continual state of growth; the tips die and dry out, while the living part of the leaf remains sturdy even in the strongest winds. One of the largest individuals possesses leaves that measure almost 2 m in width and 6 m in length, half of which is living tissue. One can estimate that a plant 1 000 years old has produced some 150 m of leaf. The plant has a pivoting root which can reach 3 m and a very wide lateral root system just under the ground surface. The *Welwitschia* can therefore absorb moisture left on the ground by fog. Yet it is also capable of absorbing water that condenses on the surface of its leaves. The seeds, on the other hand, need rain to germinate.

Dead plants can also absorb moisture during foggy nights. It has been recorded that dried grass containing less than 10% of water during the day can absorb up to 25% water by the end of the night. The gemsbok and the ostrich, which feed on these dried plants before dawn, benefit from this far from negligible source of water.

**Mesembryanthetium cryptantum**

*T*he speed of travel the Himbas show, despite the heat and rocky, difficult terrain, is altogether remarkable. The women have charge and the pace is relentless. If guardianship of the herd falls indifferently to man or woman, usually the men and male teenagers take the lead. In the desert, life is raw and each one must stand on his own.

*I*n Kaokoland, finding water remains the primary preoccupation. The search for water falls on the shoulders of the women and the quest often takes on the character of a forced march. To protect themselves from wildlife, the huts are often constructed a few hundred metres from the water source. Before retrieving water from the Kunene River, the women throw stones in to scare off the crocodiles that infest it.

## DELIGHTS OF WATER

# OCEAN OF LIFE

The Namib is a coastal desert and is bordered its full length by an exceptional marine area: the Benguela system, one of the most productive marine areas in the world. The majority of marine life in these productive waters is microscopic phytoplankton, which, needing light to thrive, is found near the surface (the euphotic zone). Phytoplankton live on carbon dioxide and nutrients (nitrates, phosphates, silicates etc.) found in the water, and sunlight to photosynthesize. Their lifespan is brief, and after death their bodies concentrate on the ocean floor where bacteria break them down into nutritive elements that enrich the deeper

nutrients, welled up along the coast. Thus the phenomenon of upwelling occurs.

Along the Namib Desert, the continental shelf is exceptionally deep, resulting in the presence of deep water close inshore. Variations in wind speed and direction, the depth of the shelf, as well as the shape of the coastline, all influence the upwelling phenomenon. The water which is pumped up to the surface comes from a depth of about 300 m in the Benguela system, thus is particularly cold. This deeper water is especially rich in nutrients, and thanks to the sunshine, provides ideal conditions for the development of dense phytoplankton growth.

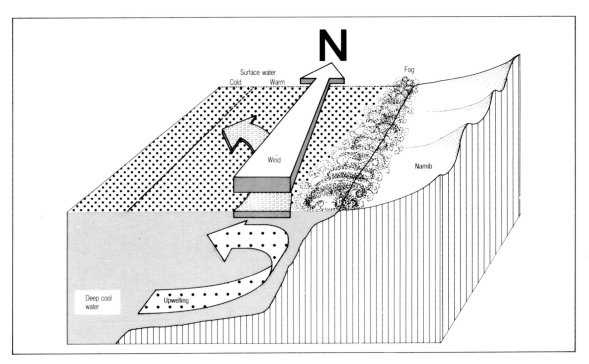

water. At such depths, through, due to the lack of light, these nutritive elements cannot be utilized.

Southerly winds, which tend to be the most violent along the coast, push surface water northward. The Coriolis force, generated by the rotation of the earth, deflects any moving object leftward in the southern hemisphere, and the oceanic water is no exception to this rule. As a result, surface water moving north is pushed out to the open sea, a phenomenon known as Eckman's transport. This water is then replaced by deeper ocean water, rich in

This high primary production constitutes the base of the marine food chain. From this abundant food source, zooplankton will develop and in turn support large shoals of pilchard, mackerel, hake, predatory fish, seals, cetaceans and sea birds.

The end of October announces the beginning of the seal's breeding season. The adult males gradually emerge from the sea which has sustained them for nearly a year, to begin their long fast. They are well prepared for the next phase of their life cycle, having accumulated a thick layer of fat beneath their dense fur. As their number grows on shore, they become increasingly aggressive and territorial scuffles break out ever more frequently. The stakes are high but of small physical size, a territory of only about 40 square metres which each male of 200 to 300 kg fights to control as his "home" for reproduction.

By mid-November females have already begun to aggregate. Less than 24 hours after her arrival, a female will give birth to a single young, covered in silky black fur, bleating like a lamb. This voice engraves itself in the memory of the mother as, for the next 10 months, it will often be the only recognizable feature of her offspring among the thousands or tens of thousands of hungry seal pups looking to nurse.

The din of the colony soon drowns out the boom of enormous Atlantic waves that pound the rocks. In early December the density of the colony reaches its maximum: 5 000 individuals per hectare. The cries of 50 000 pups merge with the mothers' responses and the bellows of competing males. Only one week after birth, the females come into oestrus and, in the midst of this crowd, each male mates with the females in his territory.

By early January, the last females have given birth; the males weakened by more than two months of incessant competition and many matings under the merciless sun of the Namib Desert, are little more than shadows of their former selves. The layer of fat under their skin has disappeared and the fur itself, soiled and streaked with blood, hangs on them like baggy overcoats. The jackals and brown hyenas are attracted by this amazing concentration of animals along the desolate coast, and tirelessly patrol the colony, stripping the carcasses of unlucky pups, seizing the weak and injured. The females have already begun their feeding routine, three days fishing at sea and one day suckling their pup. This routine will last 10 months.

The hormonal balance of the female seal changes radically at the beginning of April. The fertilized egg she has been carrying since December and which has remained dormant, suddenly begins to develop. It implants in the wall of the uterus and the placenta forms. By the end of August the female is devoting more energy to the new unborn life within her, returning less and less often to the colony, while her pup makes increasing forays into the ocean, attempting to fish, but without great success at first. The female's feeding of her pup, by the end of October, is completely halted, as she is saving her energies for the approaching birth. The young seal is already familiar with the sea and must now feed itself. It may not return to the colony for several years, until it is mature. The old males have resumed their vigilance of the colony, faithful to their annual rendezvous.

And so ends a year in the life of the seals of Cape Cross.

Approximately half a million seals inhabit the coast of Namibia, and yearly they give birth to 150 000 pups in about 15 colonies. Only 5 of these colonies are found on the continent, the rest are located on small rocky islands just offshore. The islands not used by seals shelter colonies of 20 000 pairs of Cape gannets, 45 000 pairs of Jackass penguins and 200 000 pairs of cormorants. In the surrounding waters, sea birds coming from the Antarctic and the southern ocean rendezvous with birds flying in from the Arctic. The doorstep of Namibia is the meeting point for them all.

Some years when meteorological conditions in the South Atlantic vary and prevailing southerly winds fail, the upwelling ceases, the Benguela current slows and a surface sheet of tropical warm water overruns the coast. The temperature rises noticeably, and with the failure of the upwelling, the source of nutrients is removed and the food chain falters. The shoals of fish disperse or migrate, and fish larvae suffer high mortality due to the lack of plankton. The birds desert their colonies and the seals, suffering malnutrition, suckle their pups only with difficulty and they die off in the thousands. For a while the fragile equilibrium of the ecosystem is shaken.

**Cape gannets display**

## BIRD'S PARADISE

*T*he presence of important bird colonies gave birth in the 19th century to the exploitation of guano. No longer so valued commercially, guano is still collected on artificial platforms where the mingled colours of cormorants and pelicans create surreal designs. Situated at the foot of the dunes, the lagoon of Sandwich Harbour is without a doubt one of the most magical places on the Namib coast. Pink flamingoes, permanent residents of this coastal paradise, grace this magic with their silhouettes. This strange bird has a long, flexible neck that allows it to seize shellfish, seaweed or molluscs in the lagoon. After placing its neck perpendicularly into the water, the flamingo lifts its head and uses the underside of its beak to stir up the mud. Alert to the slightest sound, the black wings unfurl and in a concert of piercing cries, the feathers meld in a flight of colours.

*I*n the bush, the passage of elephants is unmistakable. Their quiet yet devastating size and strength flatten the undergrowth. As high as 4 metres and with a mass of 6 tons, the elephant fears no one, except perhaps man. Due to his endurance, the elephant can adapt to various milieux, even the difficult environment of Kaokoland. Here we can finally see him range freely, yet protected, and rejoice in meeting him.

*A*dornment is the distinctive sign of different levels in tribal society, thus each new phase of life brings with it a transformation in external appearance. In defining the rules of adornment, the tribe assures its cohesion as well as the assumption that beauty is impossible to dissociate from tradition. The wearing of a piece of jewellery is permitted only after an initiation rite, and thus becomes a privilege. The Himbas have made their bodies a living expression of their culture and have developed an art compatible with the constraints of a nomadic people.

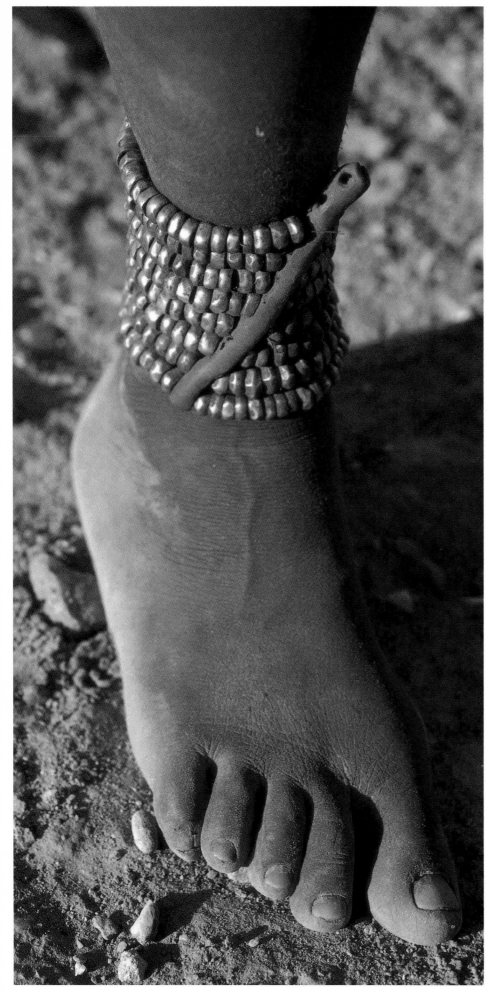

$Y$oung girls wear two large braids until the age of ten. When they reach puberty the two braids are replaced by a multitude of tresses that fall over their eyes.

After the rites celebrating a young girl's entrance into adolescence, the coiffure is tied back. This new hairstyle signifies that she has reached marriageable age. Upon marrying, the women change their hairstyle for the last time, adopting **erembe**. The length of braids, a sign of beauty, is often artificially increased with vegetable fibres.

*F*or married women, this shell (**ohumba**) is a fertility symbol. Women also wear large collars in red copper (**ondengura**) and all wear a series of pendants in metal or braided leather, from which they can hang the precious shells. The Himbas do not work in iron, so they trade with other tribes such as the Thwa to procure the material needed for their jewellery.

*T*he **ekori** is a traditional hairstyle of young married

women, which is assumed usually after the birth of the first

child. Worn during important ceremonies, the **ekori** is less

and less common today and this old man seems to be casting

a nostalgic eye to the past.

*K*aokoland is divided into 26 wards, each under the authority of a Headman. Vetamuna is the Headman of Etangwa. Often sedentary, the village chiefs have been the target for SWAPO reprisals in its war of liberation from the South African presence in Namibia. Soldiers in SWAPO attempt to discourage what they consider collaboration between the tribal chiefs and the Pretoria government. The South African army has engaged Himbas as trackers, because in this rocky and mountainous terrain the bushmen meet their match.

*M*achine guns are today part of daily life and appear in the smallest village. During migration the young boys bravely carry the artillery; symbols of change, cartridges become supplementary ornament on traditional clothing.

*C*hingui, Ovireva's Headman, as well as Vetamuna,
uses mercenaries, machine guns and mortars to protect
himself. Far from civilization, the Himbas have
preserved their secular tradition. Confrontation with
the modern world comes brutally in the war with
Angola which has accelerated the process of change.

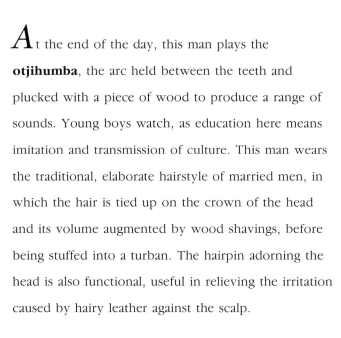

*A*t the end of the day, this man plays the **otjihumba**, the arc held between the teeth and plucked with a piece of wood to produce a range of sounds. Young boys watch, as education here means imitation and transmission of culture. This man wears the traditional, elaborate hairstyle of married men, in which the hair is tied up on the crown of the head and its volume augmented by wood shavings, before being stuffed into a turban. The hairpin adorning the head is also functional, useful in relieving the irritation caused by hairy leather against the scalp.

The Himba social structure is remarkable, and even more so that of the Herero, for the equal power held by both the matrilineal and patrilineal lines of descent: the maternal hereditary line, that of the *eanda* (pl. *omaanda*), by nature matrilineal, and that of the *oruzo*, which is patrilineal. It is the collective belief that an individual inherits the blood of his mother and the spirit of his father, a belief which defines the respective functions of matrilineal and patrilineal clans. Property rights, inheritance and economic power are all controlled by the matrilineal line of descent (privileges of the utmost importance in a pastoral society), while spiritual and political power are transmitted via the patrilineal. Placement in a matrilineal clan is of particular importance also in the social structure, as family relationships between individuals are determined according to bonds in the maternal line. The very specialized functions of each descent group (a social organization known as "Full Double Descent") result in a strong tribal organization which prevents the Himbas from being easily absorbed by modern civilization.

## THE CLAN ORGANIZATION

Among the Himbas, there exist 7 matrilineal clans, the majority of which are distributed over a vast geographic area. These clans, extending from the Hereros of Botswana to the Kuvale of Angola, all claim common descent from a singular myth of origin, the protagonists of which, all female, symbolize female descent and social organization. The name of the original mother is unknown; rather, it is the names of her daughters and granddaughters which identify the clans, each a symbolic evocation of a narrative event in the foundation myth of that clan. Thus a clan name often represents a natural element, such as the sun, the water (divisible into the rain and the spring), or a particular aspect of life fundamental in the worship.

The matrilineal clans appear to be quite ancient, predating the migration of the Hereros in the mid-16th century. The subgroup, Wonjuwo onene ("of the great house") of the clan Omukwendata, appeared then to retain and transmit vestiges of royal power, a prerogative which proves the pre-existence of a single originating matrilineal system. This prerogative is now relegated to memory in name alone, an event frequently consequent upon the introduction of patrilineal clans.

The Himbas also identify 13 patrilineal clans, or *oruzo*, each of which claims a male founder; thus, in distinction from the matrilineal clans *(omaanda)*, these 13 clans claim no common ancestry. The idea of collective origin through an original progenitor being absent in the *oruzo*, each clan cites an imaginary founder as having bequeathed to the clan its name and its concert of magico-religious taboos. It is these

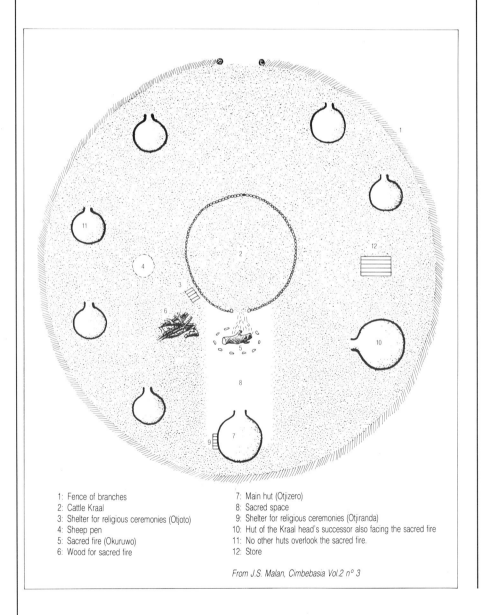

1: Fence of branches
2: Cattle Kraal
3: Shelter for religious ceremonies (Otjoto)
4: Sheep pen
5: Sacred fire (Okuruwo)
6: Wood for sacred fire
7: Main hut (Otjizero)
8: Sacred space
9: Shelter for religious ceremonies (Otjiranda)
10: Hut of the Kraal head's successor also facing the sacred fire
11: No other huts overlook the sacred fire.
12: Store

*From J.S. Malan, Cimbebasia Vol.2 n° 3*

# DESCENT

The Himba huts are made of flexible (Mopane) saplings.

taboos, the communal observance of interdictions, which define the voice and power of each clan. Yet, similar to the unnamed original mother of the matrilineal clans, the foundation epic of the oruzo is not very explicit. Rather, the myths relating the foundation of the taboos are about animals.

The taboos of the *oruzo* are, to be precise, a number of specific prescriptions under the guise of interdiction; for example, it is forbidden to possess an animal of a certain colour or to eat certain cuts of meat. There exists no identification with, or ritual devoted to, the animal in question, which would characterize the interdiction as specifically totemistic. This is particularly evident in the clan Otjihinaruzo (literally, "which has no *oruzo*"), which imposes no taboo or other condition for membership. The Otjihinaruzo, in fact, fills the important function of integrating individuals exterior to the community into the clan organization of the Himbas. Such a clan is useful in the event of a Himba woman marrying a man of another tribe which has no *oruzo*; once the woman's husband joins the Otjihinaruzo, the son can have *oruzo*. Thus every individual receives, at birth, an *eanda* from the mother and an *oruzo* from the father.

This division of rights and privileges is evident at every level of society. Upon marrying, a woman adopts the *oruzo* of her husband and goes to live in the *kraal* [1] of her husband.

Consequently, villages appear to be made up homogeneously of the same patrilineal clan, whereas the members of a matrilineal clan are dispersed. This kind of double clan organization obviates concentration of political power and inherently impedes the formation of a centralized political system. No clan has greater authority than another, thus the lack of political centralization is mirrored in the clan level. This clan organization is reproduced at the informal level of the village: lineage, the juncture of matrilineal and patrilineal lines of descent, results in a functional family unit including five living generations — the two preceding ancestral couples (parents and grandparents); the representative of the lineage; the eldest living son; and his son and grandson. The first and second generation, which is to say the originating generations, may be dead but are still considered integral members of the group. These two originating ancestors determine the living representative of the line who, according to the matrilineal rules of descent, is the heir of the herd and economic benefits of the herd. According to the patrilineal line of descent of father to son, this representative also preserves the religious functions.

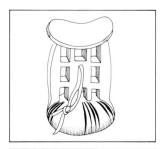

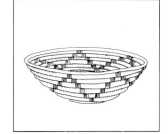

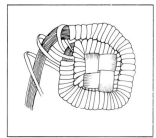

## THE HEADMEN

The chief representative of the clan is then, in effect, the head of a large family, yet the number of clan chiefs makes resolution of patrimonial and religious disputes virtually impossible. The Himbas responded to the potential dangers inherent in this multiplicity by electing a chief of clan representatives, a Headman, a kind of supreme authority to whom all individual chiefs could turn. At present, the Himbas have 26 Headmen, though the number has varied in the course of their history; each is responsible for a geographic sector within which the Headman moderates disputes. The Headmen constitute a superstructure of matrilineal clans, the name translatable literally as "the organizer of matrilineal clans." The Headmen are elected by the whole Himba people and the post is not hereditary, as such hereditary transmission of power would be inconsistent with the system of double descent.

(1) kraal designates the enclosure for the herd, but by extension, applies to the entire village.

*T*he village assembles
around one or two huts,
and the women smoke
more eagerly than the men,
pulling on their pipes with
delectation. The Himbas
borrow freely from their
environment the materials
necessary to make
everyday objects. Tanned
goat skin serves equally
well to make shirts,
headdresses or collars, and
straps for tying. Various
utensils are cut from local
trees. The strength and
flexibility of the wood
determine specific uses.

# RED TWILIGHT
# IN THE QUIET NAMIB

PALE GRASS BENDS
IN THE BREEZE IN COUNTERPOINT
TO THE NATURAL UNDULATIONS
OF THE GLOWING RED SAND.

The idea of God, in the Judeo-Christian sense of the term, does not exist among the Himbas; rather, the primary religious figure of their culture is known by three names, Ndyambi, Karunga and Huku — titles common among many of the tribes of south-western Africa. He is the creator of the world but does not intervene in the affairs of men. The first missionaries and ethnologists reported hearing the title Mukuru as the figure to whom the Himbas often made reference, but this term means "the ancient one" rather than "God."

Vetamuna, the headman of Etanga, tasting the milk.

Mukuru could as easily refer to an impersonal spiritual force as designate a respected and prestigious old man. Mukuru corresponds to the major deity of Melanesian tribes, in that he makes tangible a complex abstraction that comprehends both the ancestors and their mythic deeds, as well as the manifestations of a numinous realm peopled by invisible and inexplicable forces. The Himbas do not personify natural elements or believe in demons, and Mukuru does not appear to preserve vestiges of an original monotheism. As an impersonal force, Mukuru does not have a cult; rather, he leads a concrete hierarchy of spiritual powers, the ancestors, who are endowed with power by Mukuru to make their presence known and felt in the lives of their descendants. In his capacity as spiritual progenitor of the clans, then, Mukuru has an important role in the social structure.

### AROUND THE SACRED FIRE

The sacred fire is of fundamental importance in the rituals of the Himbas, constituting the spiritual life of a lineage and symbolizing continuity between the dead and the living. The fire is lit in a traditional way with the two "sacred sticks" *(ozondume)*: the first stick is placed horizontally, the second is fitted vertically into a hole in it and turned until sparks form. Only the chief of the line is authorized to cut and handle these sacred sticks, which he guards in his hut. The fire must never be allowed to die, preserving as it does a communication link between the ancestors and their descendants. And any breach in the conduct of the ritual is perceived as a sign of future misfortune and an offence against the ancestors.

The fire is maintained in a designated place which is also sacred, because it marks the geographic point of contact with the ancestral spirits. Not only rituals devoted to the cult of ancestors, but also all ceremonial rites of initiation are conducted around the fire which is surrounded by a circle of stones and burns from a single log. Outside the stone circle, on a rock, lies a pile of branches with which to light other important fires on ceremonial occasions. These branches, as well as the sacred sticks, come exclusively from a local tree, the mopane. The tree is often cited in legends and it is from the mopane that the subclan, Womutati, were born from the Omukweyuva.

The sacred fire and the surrounding area are located between the entrance to the central *kraal* and the entrance to the chief's hut. The only other hut to face the sacred fire is that of the clansman who will succeed the chief. All other huts are oriented away from the fire, as the village plan demonstrates.

Other ritual objects of the Himbas include a wooden bowl in which the chief mixes together water and mopane leaves, which he holds in his mouth then spits out. This ritual is repeated each time the chief of the *kraal* wants to attract the attention of the ancestral spirits and make a request.

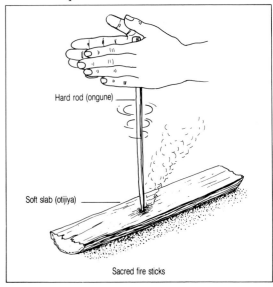

Hard rod (ongune)

Soft slab (otijiya)

Sacred fire sticks

# SOCIAL STRUCTURES

Guardianship of the sacred fire devolves upon the chief's wife, as all domestic fires in the village are lit from this single source. The area where the fire is kept is thus the central focus of village life. All rites of passage are conducted here in order to assure protection of the clan members. Certain of the sacred cattle belong to the ancestors, and specific rituals are accordingly conducted there, such as the initiation rite of the new chief, who lays a heifer on the tomb of the previous chief, slashes its ear, then sacrifices the animal to the ancestral spirits. A small amount of milk from the sacrificial cow is also poured on the tomb. On returning to the *kraal*, the new chief pours more milk on the sacred fire, then tastes some himself. The ritual complete, other members of the clan may drink of the milk.

The chief may declare any animal sacred, thus there exist a number of important categories of sacred cattle, each with its own rituals and taboos. The sacred animal belongs to the *oruzo* and its inheritance is along the patrilineal line. Upon the death of a chief, his religious functions are assumed by a brother, who can maintain the direct line with paternal ancestry of father and grandfather. If problems of grazing necessitate a division of the group, only a brother of the chief can establish a new *kraal*, as he is empowered to conduct the religious rites. In all cases, a son of a *kraal* chief, so long as an uncle is living, may not establish a new village; it is only after the death of all third generation males that the leadership may pass on to the next generation, the great grandson of the originating ancestor.

## MAGIC PRACTICES

Apart from religious practices, the Himbas, like all primitive peoples, have recourse to magic; divination and shamanism are two functions met principally by the Zemba and the Hakaona, tribes of southern Angola. The common definition of divination is the prediction of the future or explication of past events by inspection of animal entrails. When a goat is killed or a steer sacrificed, the *ombetere*, often an old woman, interprets the veins and configurations of the stomach to make predictions. In cases of illness or common suffering, the *ombetere* seeks the causes of the ill, various rites surrounding the consultation. Proposed remedies can include sacrifices around the sacred fire and divinations themselves, which offer the possi-

**Vetamuna in the *Okurowo* (sacred fire).**

bility for direct consultation with the ancestors. The *onanga* (shaman) may be called to cure some illnesses or instances of possession.

The Himbas also enjoy perfect familiarity with herbal remedies and magic: medical (leaves of the mopane to stop haemorrhage); religious (chopped roots which facilitate communication with the spirits); magical (leaves which make a crocodile release his prey); hygienic and cosmetic (vegetation used in perfume or as soap).

$L$ife without the raising of cattle has no meaning for the Himbas. Accumulation of a herd is the end of life. Goats and cattle do not, though, have the same function. The goat is utilitarian, while the cow is a mark of prestige. At the centre of each village the **kraal**, a wooden enclosure, protects the calves. The

**kraal** is also the sacred point that unites the tribe with the herd ; it is the social and religious heart of the village. Part of the herd is sacred and no cow can be sacrificed except for important rites such as marriage or burial. Only the milk is consumed, and forms the basis of the diet.

*A*ll of a sudden the sky clouds over and the miraculous vision of the first few drops of rain in the desert appears. Little accustomed to this gift from heaven, the parched earth is incapable of absorbing the water, so in minutes lakes form in the dunes, and the light assumes a strange quality, as a rainbow refracts the voluptuous forms of the sand hills. The horizon lowers and the first cries of jackals announce the onset of the African night.

*I*n the tender late afternoon, the animals come back to life. The hooves of the oryx and springbok kick up columns of dust in a sky that promises the much

hoped-for rain. In this immense sea of sand the dunes

meld form and colour into deceptive shadows and

light, creating a new image each instant.

$O$ff Diaz Point, the silent
sun retreats into the crashing
waves. The seals continue to
call and on Halifax Island near
the coast, the penguins flee into
the shadows as if starring in a
silent movie run at top speed.
Night embraces the earth but
not all surrender to Morpheus.

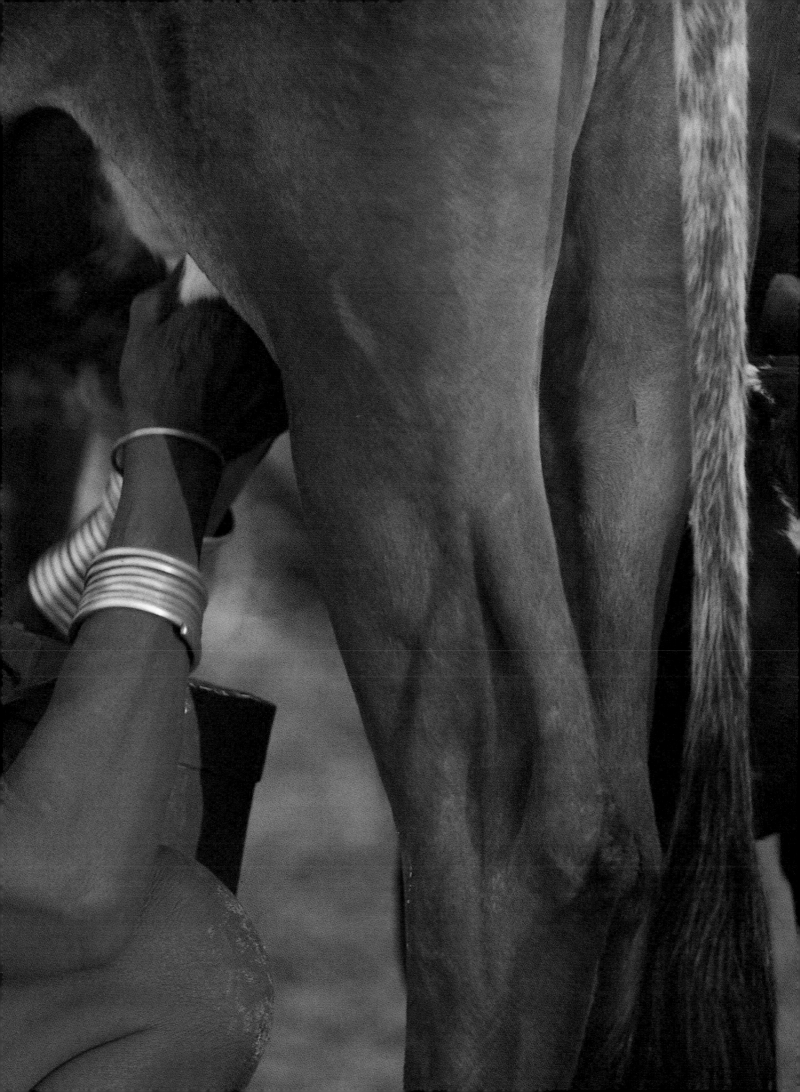

*F*rom atop the escarpment 1500m above the Marienfluss Valley, the Himbas can see their past and their future. This wide valley of red sand leads to both the Kunene River and Angola. This evening, as every evening, the herd is collected and the Himbas can say « Nawa, » « Perinawa » — all is well. Tomorrow, they must depart and follow the clouds again, hoping for the next rain. I long to share their immutable traditions, indifference to civilization. I dream and hope their obstinacy will suffice to keep the modern world at bay.

# BIBLIOGRAPHY

## DESERT

BRANCH B. , Field guide to the snakes and other reptiles of Southern Africa, Struik Cape Town 1988.
COLE D.T., Lithops. Flowering stones. Acorn Books. Randburg 1988.
CRAVEN P. & MARAIS C., Namib flora. Gamsberg Cape Town 1986.
LOUW G.N. & SEELY M.K., Ecology of desert organisms. Longman London 1982.
NEWMAN K., Birds of Southern Africa. Macmillan Johannesburg 1983.
PAYNE A. I. L. & CRAWFORD R. M. J., Oceans of life Southern Africa Vlaeberg Cape Town 1989.
REARDON M. & REARDON M., Etosha, life and death on an African plain. Struik Cape Town 1981.
REARDON M., The besieged desert. Collins 1986.
SCHOEMAN A.. Skeleton Coast. Macmillan Johannesburg 1984.
SCOLTZ C.H. & HOLM E., Insects of Southern Africa. Butterworths Durban 1986.
SKAIFE S. H., African insect life. Country life books, Hamlyn London 1979.
SMITHERS R. H.N., The Mammals of the Southern African Subregion. University of Pretoria 1983.
WAGNER F.H., Wildlife of the deserts. Chanticleer Press New York 1980.

WARD J.D., SEELY M.K. & LANCASTER N., On the antiquity of the Namib. S. Afr. J. Sci. 79: 175-183. 1983.
SEELY M. K., The Namib. Shell Oil SWA Windhoek 1987.
"Madoqua" Scientific magazine published by the Department of Nature Conservation.
HALL-MARTIN A., WALKER C. & BOTHMA J. du P, Kaokoveld — The last wilderness, Southern Book Publishers 1988.

## HIMBA

ESTERMANN C., Ethnography of south west Angola. Lisbon 1957.
MALAN J. S., Peoples of SWA Namibia. Haum Cape Town 1980
CIMBEBASIA:
Series B Vol. 2 n°4 The Herero speaking peoples of Kaokoland. MALAN 1974.
Series B Vol. 2 n°3 Double descent among the Himba of SWA. MALAN 1973.
Series B Vol. 2 n°5 The ethnobotany of Kaokoland. MALAN & OWEN-SMITH 1974.
N°13 Preliminary report of two stone-working OvaTjimba groups in the northern Kaokoveld of SWA.McCALMAN H. R. & GROBBELAAR B.J. 1965.
Notes on Kaokoveld. Ethnological publication N°26 Pretoria 1951.

# ACKNOWLEDGEMENTS:

The Department of Nature Conservation
Garth Owen-Smith (Namibia Wildlife Trust)
The director and staff of the Desert Ecological Rescarch Unit in Gobabeb
The Sea Fisheries in Cape Town and Lüderitz
Consolidated Diamond Mines in Oranjemund
We are specially indebted to Chris Eyres for his efficient help and to
Raymond Dujardin for his friendly co-operation.
We also thank all those who helped us make this volume possible:
Martin Behrtens, Alain Degré, Beith Process, Gerard Fouché,
Michel and Françoise Guignard, Dave Hardy, Helga Knieckel,
Mike and Annette Knight, John and Astrie Leroy, Catherine and Ekhart Klenkler,
Sylvie Robert, Jutta Rohwer, Jean-Paul and Suzanne Roux, Zaza and our parents.
The text is translated by Tamsin Baum.

We work with Nikon material and use Kodachrome film.

ISBN 1 86812 270 0
First edition, first impression 1989 by
Southern Book Publishers (Pty) Ltd.
P O Box 548, Bergvlei 2012
Johannesburg
Previously published by Copyright/Paris
Set by Compo-Akrour — Paris
Printed and bound in Spain
by Cronion S.A.